W9-BKR-061

ANN MORRIS

SHOES · SHOES · SHOES

LOTHROP, LEE & SHEPARD BOOKS
NEW YORK

The author wishes to thank the photographers and photo agencies who contributed the photographs (all under copyright) to this book:
Ideawright/Barry Simpson p. 2; Ann Morris p. 9, 17 top; Photo Marion-Valentine/Marion Valentine p. 19 top, 27 top; Rapho Photographique/J. M. Charles p. 26 bottom, J. E. Pasquier p. 28 left, M. Serraillier p. 14, V. Winckler p. 24 & front cover; Viesti Associates/Steve Cohen p. 7, 28 right, Martha Cooper p. 16, Claudia Dhimitri p. 15, Bill Gallery p. 10 left, Alan Kearney p. 22, Kit Kittle p. 29, Craig Lovell p. 23, Carl Rosenstein p. 20, 21, Frank Siteman page 11 left, Joe Viesti p. 1, p. 10 right, 12 bottom, 13, 17, 18 bottom; Woodfin Camp & Associates/Ken Heyman p. 5, 6, 8, 11 right, 12 top, 19 bottom, 25, 26 top, 27 bottom, back cover.

 Inquiries should be addressed to Lothrop, Lee & Shepard Books, a division of William Morrow & Company, Inc., 1350 Avenue of the Americas, New York, New York 10019.
Printed in the United States of America
First Edition 1 2 3 4 5 6 7 8 9 10
Library of Congress Cataloging in Publication Data
Morris, Ann. Shoes, shoes, shoes / by Ann Morris.
p. cm. Summary: Illustrations and simple text describe all kinds of shoes—some for dancing, walking, playing, some for snow or ice, some made of wood or cloth.
ISBN 0-688-13666-4. — ISBN 0-688-13667-2 (lib. bdg.) 1. Shoes—Juvenile literature. [1. Shoes.] I. Title.
GT2130.M67 1995 391'.413—dc20 94-46649 CIP AC

SHOES · SHOES · SHOES

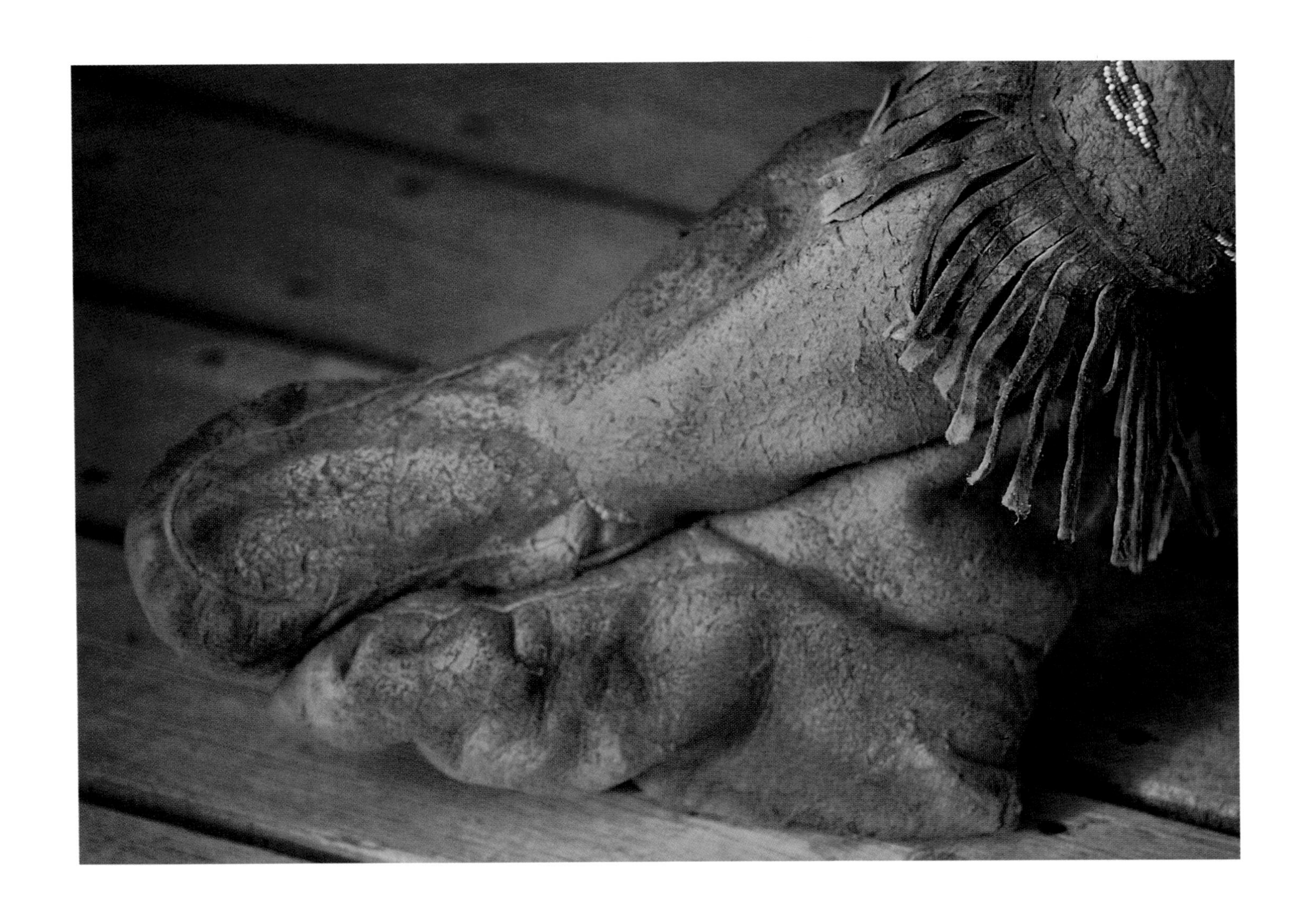

Shoes, shoes, all kinds of shoes,
wherever you find them, shoes come in twos!

Old shoes,

new shoes,

just-right-for-you shoes.

Work shoes,

play shoes,

any-time-of-day shoes.

There are school shoes

and dancing shoes,

walking shoes

and riding shoes,

shoes for the ice,

and shoes for the snow.

Shoes keep your feet dry wherever you go.

Wooden shoes,

cloth shoes,

shoes made out of straw—

All over the world, in lands near and far,

there are shoes that are right for wherever you are.

INDEX

Half title UNITED STATES: The Haines Shoe House in York, Pennsylvania, is a full-sized home built in the shape of a shoe.

Title page UNITED STATES: Watching animals with big flat feet, such as ducks, walk on top of deep snow without sinking probably gave a Native American inventor the idea for snow-shoes.

5 RUSSIA: A ballerina's slippers are specially shaped and padded so she can balance on the tips of her toes. It takes many years of hard train-ing to dance in toe shoes.

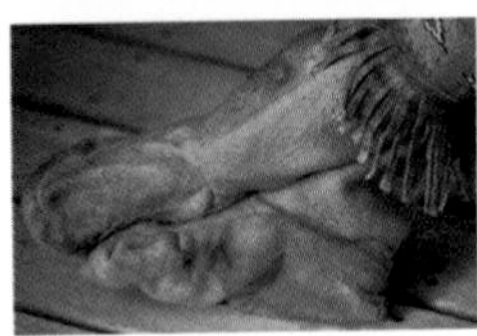

7 CANADA: Leather moccasins are soft and comfortable. *Moccasin* means shoe in Algonquian.

8 KENYA: Sandals are the oldest kind of shoe. Artwork found in the tombs of East African kings who lived thousands of years ago shows people wearing sandals.

9 NETHERLANDS: The Dutch are known for their brilliant colored tulips and wooden shoes. These are for sale at a souvenir stand in Amster-dam.

10 JAPAN: This girl is wearing a traditional kimono and wooden-soled thongs to take part in a ceremony at Asakusa Kannon Temple in Tokyo. Kannon is the goddess of Mercy.

10 GUATEMALA: In Guatemala, where this boy lives, shoes are called *los zapatos*.

11 UNITED STATES: This young girl is glad she has insulated snow boots to warm her feet after skating.

12 UNITED STATES: Most work boots have steel plates in the toes to keep you from getting hurt if something heavy falls on your foot.

12 SPAIN: Wooden sabots also protect your feet.

13 COLOMBIA: High boots are good shoes for farmers who work in fields, where they may walk on thorny plants, stinging insects, or snakes.

14 SWEDEN: Soccer players have cleats on the bottom of their shoes to help them run on slip-pery mud and grass.

15 HONG KONG: These sandals are some-times called slip-ons because they are so easy to take on and off.

16 KENYA: Masai dancing features spectacular leaps. Thick-soled sandals help cushion the landing.

17 BOLIVIA: Rubber-soled sandals and sneakers are good shoes for street musicians who are on their feet all day.

18 MEXICO: Black leather shoes are required with this school uniform.

18 COLOMBIA: Athletic shoes are perfect for running on hard surfaces, such as this paved playground where students are beginning a race.

19 UNITED STATES: This Navajo father is teaching his children a traditional dance.

19 ROMANIA: In this folk dance, the men jump over their canes. Because their shoes have smooth soles that curve up in front, the dancers toes don't catch on the canes.

20 MOROCCO: This woman lives in the desert city of Essaouira. Her open-toed mules let sand run out as she walks.

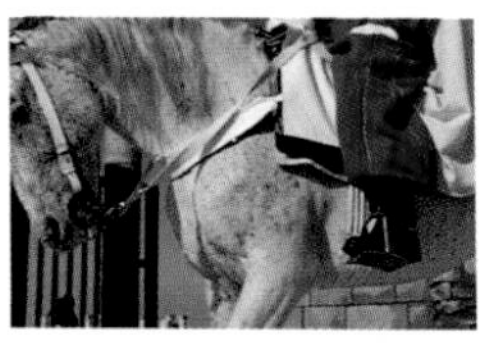

21 MOROCCO: This royal guard to the King of Morocco must polish his riding boots every day to keep them shiny.

22 UNITED STATES: Metal talons lashed to the bottom of his hiking boots help this adventurer climb straight up a wall of solid ice.

23 CHINA: This father and daughter are Tibetan Sherpas, who live high in the Himalaya mountains. Their boots are designed to be warm as well as beautiful.

24 ENGLAND: Wellington boots are named after the English Duke of Wellington, who liked to wear knee-high boots. Red waterproof "wellies" are the perfect shoes for visiting a friend on a rainy day.

25 UNITED STATES: Fire fighters' boots are water- *and* fireproof. The boots are loose so they can be pulled on in a hurry.

26 JAPAN: These wooden sandals are often worn with special socks called *tabi* that separate the big toe from the rest.

26 NETHERLANDS: Carving wooden shoes by hand takes patience and skill.

27 CHINA: The Forbidden City in Beijing, where these old friends are taking a rest, was once the home of Chinese Emperors.

28 ITALY: A proud mother and grandmother help this baby break in her new shoes.

28 THAILAND: The saffron-colored robe identifies this young man as a buddhist monk.

Where in the world were these photographs taken?

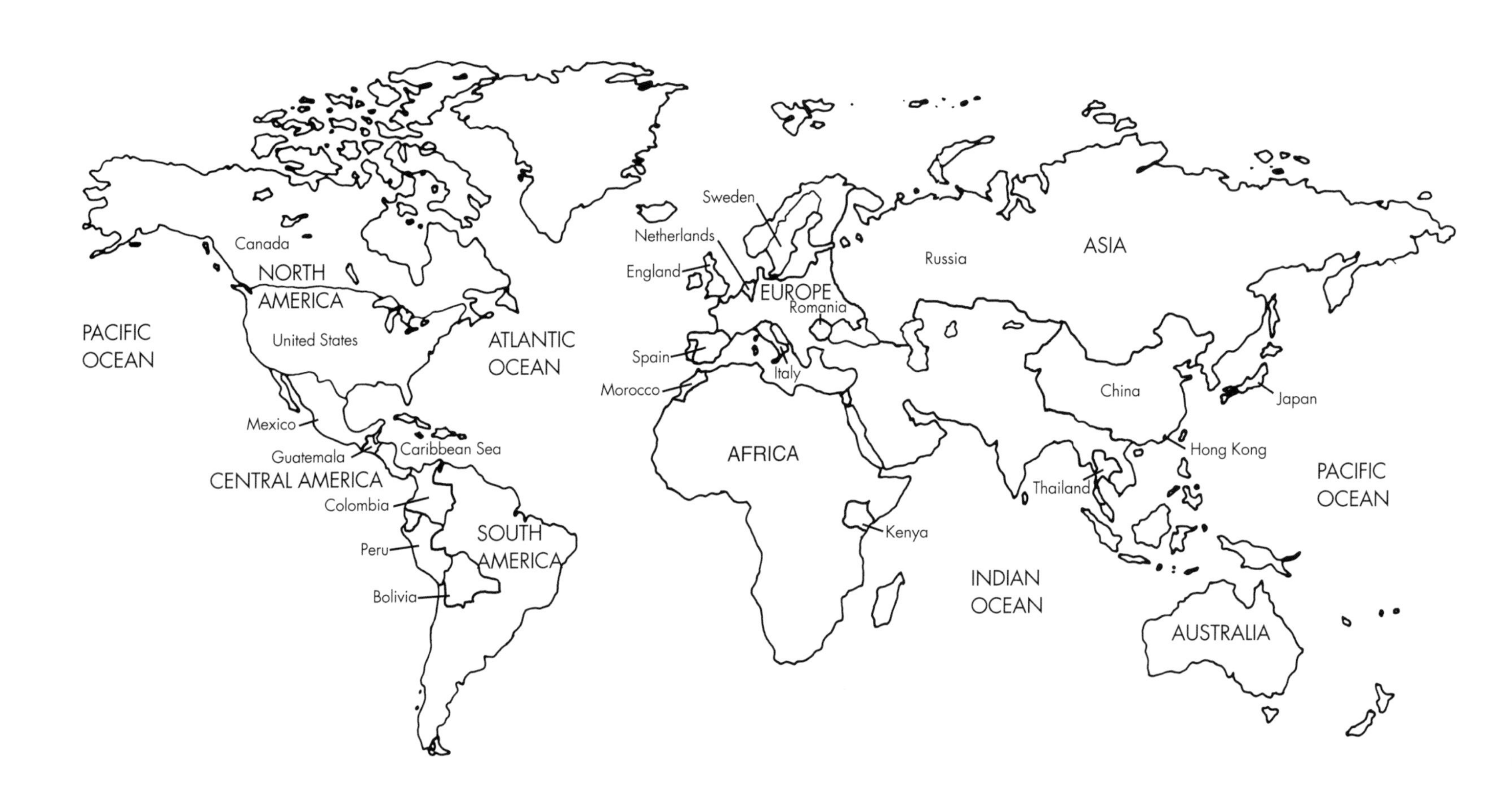

FRANKLIN PIERCE COLLEGE LIBRARY
00093767